# I have a rhyme,
# My Body is Mine

© 2020 Nur Choudhury
All rights reserved.
No part of this publication may be reproduced
or transmitted in any form or by any means,
electronic or mechanical, including photocopying,
recording, or any information storage
or retrieval system, without permission in writing
from the author.

Written by Nur Choudhury
Illustrations by Jennifer Pacuma
www.involvedfathers.com

Page 1

I have **eyes** and a **nose** and parts that are hidden by my clothes.

Some parts you can see and others are just for me.

Page 3

They are my private parts and you have them too. Your private parts belong to no one else but you.

Page 5

"No secrets", is something mum and dad say. If I ever felt hurt I would tell them without delay.

Page 7

I visited my cousin's house last week. We were playing a game of hide and seek.

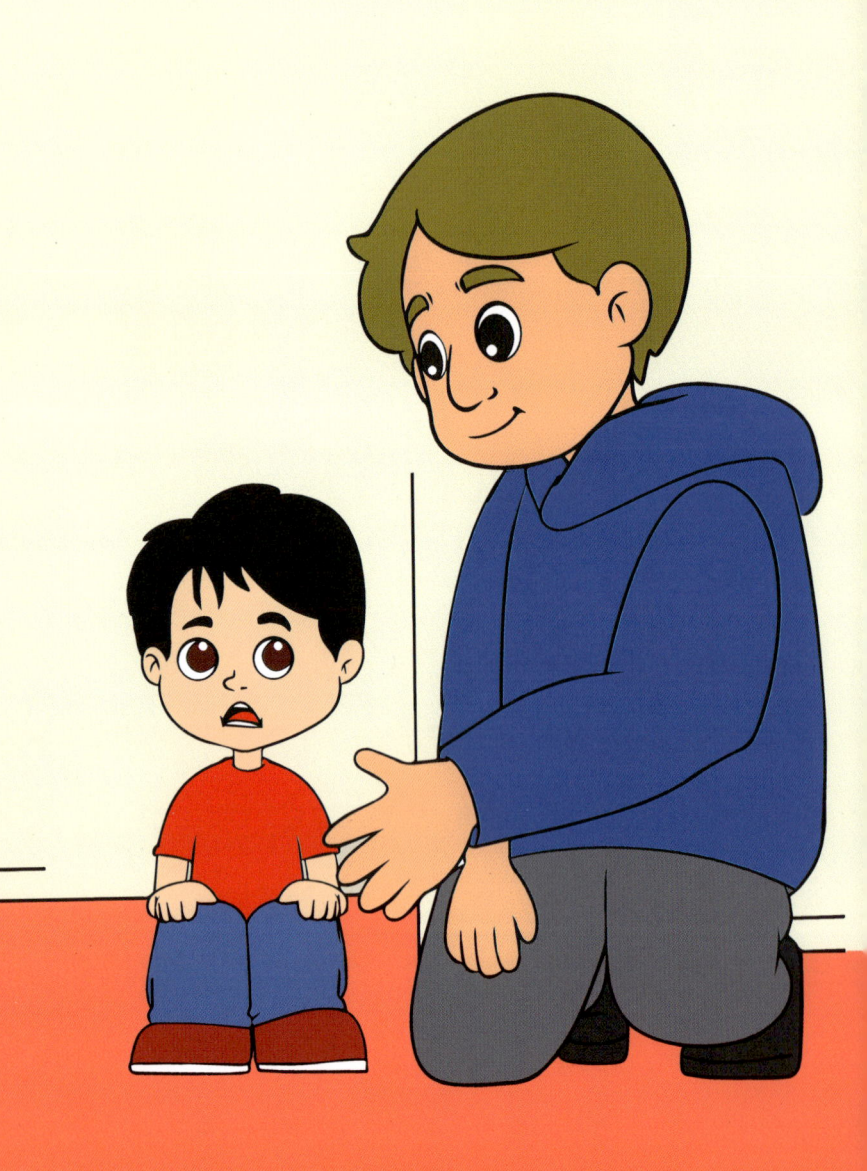

Page 9

As I hid away behind

the paintings and art.

Someone came

and touched my

private part.

Page 11

I was shocked and scared as a tear rolled down my face. I kept on thinking my body is mine, why did you have to touch my private place?

Page 13

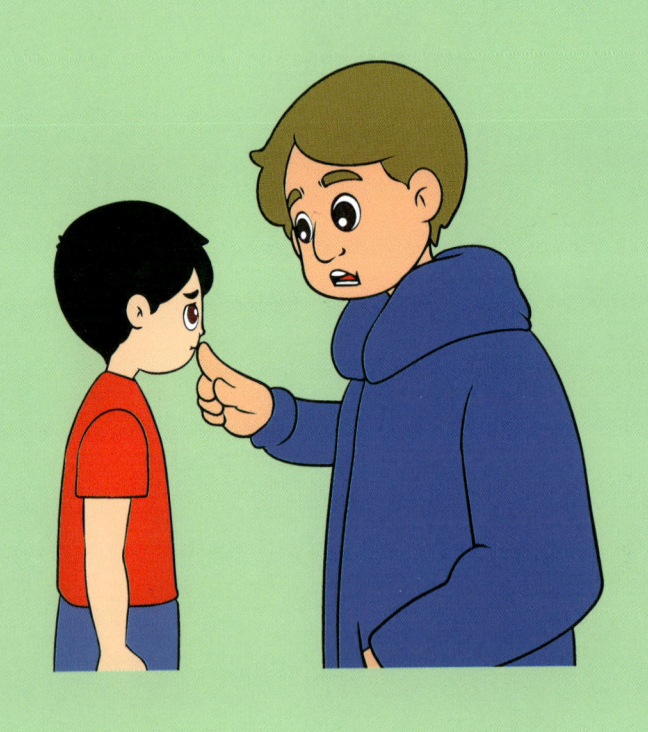

I stood there afraid as this person whispered into my ear. "It will be our little secret, don't go anywhere."

Page 15

I ran away screaming

NO NO NO.

I hugged

mum and dad

and told them so.

Page 17

No Secrets, do you remember mum and dad? Something just happened and I feel really bad.

Page 19

They hugged me tight

and kissed my cheek.

They said I was so

brave to tell them, that

I deserved a treat.

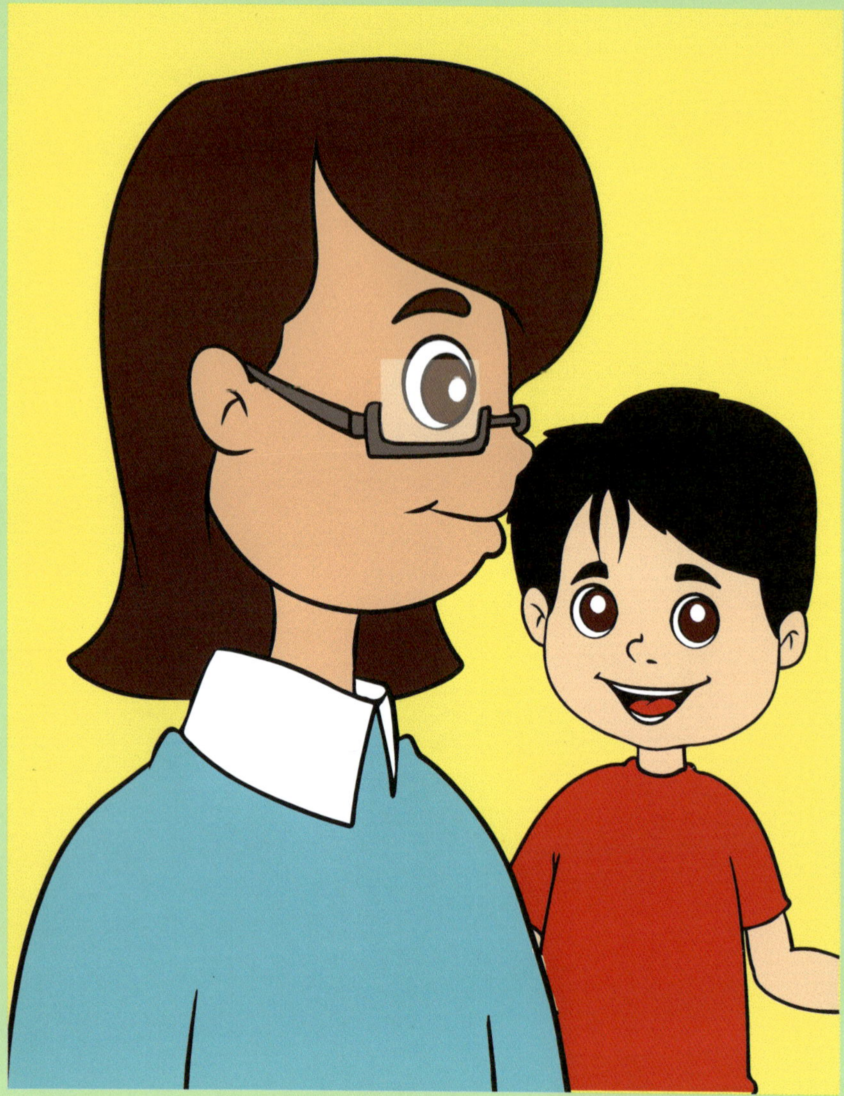

I want to share something with you that's really cool. You can also tell a teacher when you're at school.

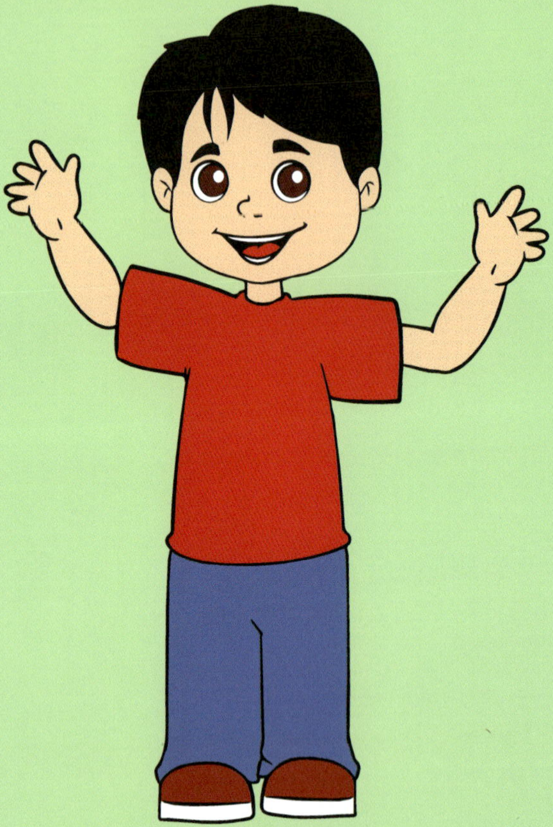

Some things you can't keep a secret and that's fine. Everything's going to be OK because my body is mine.

# FOLLOW ON QUESTIONS FOR PARENTS, CARERS, AND TEACHERS TO ASK OR DISCUSS.

WHAT SIGNS OR FEELINGS DOES OUR BODY GIVE US THAT SOMETHING MIGHT BE UNSAFE?

WHAT REACTIONS MIGHT WE HAVE WHEN WE FEEL UNSAFE?

WHO IS ALLOWED TO SEE YOUR PRIVATE PARTS?

SOME SECRETS CAN BE NICE SURPRISES (SAFE SECRETS) BUT SOME ARE NOT-SO-NICE AND MAY EVEN BE UNSAFE LIKE THE ONE MENTIONED IN THE BOOK. CAN YOU THINK OF SOME SAFE SECRETS (NICE SURPRISES)?

CAN YOU THINK OF OTHER NOT-SO-NICE SECRETS?

CAN YOU NAME 5 ADULTS THAT YOU CAN TRUST TO TELL THEM IF SOMETHING BAD HAS HAPPENED TO YOU, ONE FOR EACH FINGER ON YOUR HAND?

Printed in Great Britain
by Amazon